*Sometimes it still amazes me —
how I get so anxious and thrilled
and thoughtful about you; I guess
maybe it's because I just keep
falling wonderfully in love with
you... over and over again.*

— Jamie Delere

# Blue Mountain Arts®

*Bestselling Books*

*By Susan Polis Schutz:*
*To My Daughter, with Love, on the Important Things in Life*
*To My Son, with Love*
*I Love You*

*100 Things to Always Remember... and One Thing to Never Forget*
*by Alin Austin*

*Is It Time to Make a Change?*
*by Deanna Beisser*

*To The Love of My Life*
*by Donna Fargo*

*Chasing Away the Clouds*
*To the One Person I Consider to Be My Soul Mate*
*by Douglas Pagels*

*For You, Just Because You're Very Special to Me*
*by Collin McCarty*

*Being a Teen ...Words of Advice from Someone Who's Been There*
*by Diane Mastromarino*

*girls rule ...a very special book created especially for girls*
*by Ashley Rice*

*A Lifetime of Love ...Poems on the Passages of Life*
*by Leonard Nimoy*

*Anthologies:*
*42 Gifts I'd Like to Give to You*
*Always Believe in Yourself and Your Dreams*
*A Daughter Is Forever*
*For You, My Daughter*
*Friends for Life*
*I Love You, Mom*
*I'm Glad You Are My Sister*
*The Joys and Challenges of Motherhood*
*The Language of Recovery ...and Living Life One Day at a Time*
*May You Always Have an Angel by Your Side*
*Take Each Day One Step at a Time*
*Teaching and Learning Are Lifelong Journeys*
*There Is Greatness Within You, My Son*
*These Are the Gifts I'd Like to Give to You*
*Think Positive Thoughts Every Day*
*Thoughts to Share with a Wonderful Teenager*
*To My Child*
*With God by Your Side ...You Never Have to Be Alone*

# I Keep Falling in Love with You

A Blue Mountain Arts® Collection

**Blue Mountain Press**™

SPS Studios, Inc., Boulder, Colorado

We wish to thank Susan Polis Schutz for permission to reprint the following poems that appear in this publication: "In my dreams...," "As time goes by...," "More than ever...," and "When we first met...." Copyright © 1983 by Stephen Schutz and Susan Polis Schutz. All rights reserved.

Library of Congress Catalog Card Number: 2001002810
ISBN: 0-88396-198-9

ACKNOWLEDGMENTS appear on page 64.

Certain trademarks are used under license.

Manufactured in the United States of America.

Third printing of this edition: July 2002

 This book is printed on recycled paper.

This book is printed on fine quality, laid embossed, 80 lb. paper. This paper has been specially produced to be acid free (neutral pH) and contains no groundwood or unbleached pulp. It conforms with all the requirements of the American National Standards Institute, Inc., so as to ensure that this book will last and be enjoyed by future generations.

### Library of Congress Cataloging-in-Publication Data

I keep falling in love with you : a Blue Mountain Arts collection.
    p. cm.
  ISBN 0-88396-198-9 (softcover : alk. paper)
  1. Love poetry, American.  I. SPS Studios (Firm)
  PS595.L6 I113 2001
  811.008'03543—dc21

2001002810
CIP

# SPS Studios, Inc.

P.O. Box 4549, Boulder, Colorado 80306

# Contents

1   Jamie Delere

7   Daniel Haughian

8   Anna Tafoya

11  Jamie Delere

12  Lindsay Newman

15  Susan Polis Schutz

16  Edmund O'Neill

19  Daniel Haughian

20  Lindsay Newman

23  Jamie Delere

24  Andrew Tawney

25  Michael J. Mulvena

25  Nathaniel Hawthorne

27  Susan Polis Schutz

28  Karen Jessie

31  Susan Polis Schutz

32  Guy de Maupassant

33  Edmund O'Neill

35  Sheri Daugherty

36  Nancy Sue Krenrich

37  Tracy L. Trainer

39  Jamie Delere

40  Edward O'Blenis

41  Richard W. Weber

43  Thomas R. Dudley

44  Margaret O'Reilly-Lahda

45  Claudia Adrienne Grandi

47  Lindsay Newman

48  Janice C. Sullivan

49  Sharon T. Salter

51  Laine Parsons

52  Jamie Delere

55  Laine Parsons

56  Donna Fargo

59  Susan Polis Schutz

60  Jacqueline Faye
    Sanderson-Mixon

63  Chris Gallatin

64  Acknowledgments

# What It's like
# to Love You

To love you is to daydream of you often, think of you so much, speak of you proudly, and miss you terribly when we are apart.

To love you is to cherish the warmth of your arms, the sweetness of your kiss, the friendliness of your smile, the loving sound in your voice, and the happiness we share.

To love you is to never forget the adversity we have overcome, the tears we have shed, the plans we have made, the problems we have solved, and the pain of separation.

To love you is to remember joyfully the days we made memorable, the moments that will live forever in our hearts, the dreams we hope for, the feelings we have for each other, the caresses and touches of love, and the exhilaration of love that fills our hearts.

To love you is to need you, want you, hold you, and know you as no one else can.

To love you is to realize that life without you would be no life at all...

That's a little of what it's like
to be in love with you!

— Daniel Haughian

# "You"

*I love having you in my life. It has never been the same since you came into it, and I know it will never be the same again.*

*I love you so much. You are always inside me, warm within my heart, and you are everywhere in the world that surrounds me. You come to me tenderly. You take my soul places it's never been before. You give me more of you than I ever knew anyone could give.*

*You give me feelings that feel like presents almost too beautiful to open. Among the gifts you have given, one of the most wonderful of all is the joy of being so close to you. Thank you for trusting me enough to share all that you are... with all that I hope to be.*

*I love catching glimpses of every new facet you share with me. And the more you do that... the more I can't help but adore what I see.*

*In the time that we have been together, you have made my sun rise on so many mornings — and I'm sure it was you who made my stars come out at night. You've surprised me with the gifts of hope and laughter and love, and you've made me a believer in something I never used to have too much faith in: the notion that dreams really can come true.*

*If there are times when you look at me and see my eyes filled with smiles and tears, it's only because my heart is so full of happiness, and because my life is so thankful for ...you.*

*— Anna Tafoya*

*I'm not sure when I first fell in love with you... I guess it could have been as early as that first time we held each other, or the first time I realized that you kind of liked me, too...*

*I'm not sure; I just remember thinking of you more and more and getting less and less done in the process! I remember wanting you to stay so badly — and being so thrilled at the thought. I remember praying that it was you whenever the phone would ring, but at the same time hoping it wasn't; because I didn't know how in the world I was going to sound romantic and impressive when what I felt was anxious and tongue-tied...*

*Sometimes it still amazes me — how I get so anxious and thrilled and thoughtful about you; I guess maybe it's because I just keep falling wonderfully in love with you... over and over again.*

*— Jamie Delere*

*Our first times*
*are the ones I remember*
*the most…*

*The first time we met*
*the first time we talked*
*the first time you called*
*and we went out*
*The first time that we*
*were separated*
*and I told you I'd miss you*
*The first time I cried when*
*you were gone*
*The first time you told me*
*that you loved me*
*the first time I said*
*"I love you"*
*and the time that we first*
*loved*

*The first time I met your*
  *family and friends*
*the first time that you*
  *met mine*
*and the first time I knew*
*that our love was going*
  *to last...*

*Between us*
*there have been many*
  *first times*
*and I remember each*
  *and every one*
*But the time I remember*
  *most often...*
*is the first time*
  *I fell in love*
    *with you*

— *Lindsay Newman*

*In my dreams*
*I pictured a person*
*who was*
*intelligent, good-looking*
*sensitive, talented*
*creative, fun*
*strong and wise*
*who would completely*
*overwhelm me*
*with love*
*Since dreams*
*can be just*
*wishful thinking*
*I did not really expect*
*to find one person*
*who had all these*
*outstanding qualities*
*But then —*
*I met you*
*and not only did you*
*bring back my*
*belief in dreams*
*but you are even*
*more wonderful*
*than my*
*dreams*

*— Susan Polis Schutz*

You and I took a special chance
the first time we met...
we both knew enough of love,
and life, to understand that
two people don't fall in love,
they grow into it, slowly —
and we'd both been hurt before
by feelings that seemed too easily lost...
but there was something between us
from the beginning, a unique harmony
that made us take that special chance...

You and I took a special chance
the first time we argued...
after feeling hurt and sad,
and both of us trying to apologize
at the same time for disagreeing
over such a small matter, we knew
that our relationship was worth more
than anything that might come between us.

*We knew after that first time*
*that what we had together*
*would see us through the hard times*
*and make us better appreciate the good,*
*because we took that special chance...*

*You and I took a special chance*
*the first time we said "I love you"...*
*for we knew that we would share*
*stormy as well as sunny times,*
*laughter and tears, some dreams that*
*would come beautifully true, and others*
*that would fade in our memories —*
*and we knew in our hearts*
*that our love deserved all the effort*
*we could make to fulfill our life together...*
*for we took that special chance...*
*    and found a very special love.*

*— Edmund O'Neill*

You have my love for
as long as you want it...
If there is anything that
   I can do
to make you happy,
then I will gladly do it,
for making you happy is
what I want my life to be about.
It is my fondest wish that
   our time together be the
most memorable time in your life.
And the love I give you today
   is the least
you can ever expect from me,
for as each new day unfolds,
my love for you increases...
because every day that I am
   in love with you
      is the greatest day
      in my life.

— Daniel Haughian

# Touched by Love

*I knew I had been touched*
*by love...*
*the first time I saw you*
*and I felt your warmth*
*and heard your laughter.*

*I knew I had been touched*
*by love...*
*when I was hurting from*
*something that happened,*
*and you came along*
*and made the hurt go away.*

*I knew I had been touched*
*by love...*
*when I quit making plans*
*with my friends*
*and started dreaming dreams*
*with you.*

*I knew I had been touched*
    *by love...*
*when I stopped thinking in*
    *terms of "me"*
*and started thinking in*
    *terms of "we."*

*I knew I had been touched*
    *by love...*
*when suddenly I couldn't make*
    *decisions by myself anymore,*
*and I had this strong desire*
*to share everything with you.*

*I knew I had been touched*
    *by love...*
*the first time we spent*
    *alone together*
*and I knew I wanted to stay*
    *with you forever...*
*because I had never felt*
    *this touched by love.*

*— Lindsay Newman*

*I* want nothing but the best for you,
and that's why I want you
to always have me in your life...

Wanting the best for you
means wanting you to always have
a friend you can count on,
    a love you can celebrate,
        arms you can come home to,
and a life that feels fulfilled.
Wanting the best for you
makes me wish that
you'll always want me in your life,
because nobody will love you like I will.
Nobody will try as hard
    to give you what you need
    and what you wish for,
and nobody could feel
    as happy as I am
    or as privileged
    or as hopeful.
I want the best for you...
and that includes me.
Not because I'm perfect...
but just because
    I'm perfectly in love with you.

— Jamie Delere

# To someone who is beautiful...
## all over

It is absolutely wonderful to have
someone in your life who is caring
and giving and gracious — someone whose
smiles are like sunshine and laughter
and whose words always seem to say
the things you most like to hear...
because those magical people are really
beautiful... inside.

And it is a special privilege to
know someone whose outward appearance
is a delight just to see — someone who
lights up a room with radiance and
who lights up my little corner of the
world with a loveliness it has never
known before... because special people
like that are really beautiful... outside.

But most of all, it is one of the
world's most special blessings to
have a person in your life who can
add so much pleasure and such magnificence
to the days — as you have to mine...
because you're someone who is beautiful...
all over.

— Andrew Tawney

What I wanted when I first knew you
was your smile.
What I wanted later
was your encouragement,
your gentle caresses,
your positive approach,
your love.
What I wanted, too, was your approval,
your pride,
your laughter.
What I wanted all along...
was you.

— Michael J. Mulvena


You are the only person
in the world
that was ever necessary
to me.

— Nathaniel Hawthorne

As time goes by
we know each other better
we share more things together
we have reached or not reached
    so many goals together
we have so many emotions and
    experiences together
As time goes by
the bonds holding us together
get stronger and stronger
the foundation of our relationship
gets stronger and stronger
my feelings of oneness with you
get stronger and stronger
As time goes by
my feeling of love for you
    gets stronger
        and stronger

— Susan Polis Schutz

*To you, my love, I vow...*

*Be my strength,*
*and I will be the same for you.*
*Like a mirror, I will reflect*
*the love you so freely give.*
*Like the infinite circles*
*that ripple forth in water*
*pierced by a stone,*
*I will radiate the happiness*
*you bring to my soul.*
*In times of darkness,*
*I will cling to the memories*
*of our unity*
*and provide you with inner visions*
*of this same bond to be your faith.*

*In times of sorrow,*
*I will be your comfort and*
*divide your grief*
*by sharing it...*
*In times of joy,*
*I will rejoice in our love*
*and encompass you with every*
*tenderness.*
*Together or apart, I will*
*cherish everything about you*
*with all my heart.*
*Be my strength,*
*and I will be the same*
*for you.*

*— Karen Jessie*

*More than ever*
*I love you*
*More than ever*
*I admire you*
*More than ever*
*I like you*
*More than ever*
*I respect you*
*More than ever*
*I want you*
*forever*

*— Susan Polis Schutz*

*I wish I could make you*
*understand how I love you.*
*I am always seeking, but*
    *cannot find a way...*

*I love in you a something*
*that only I have discovered —*
*the you which is beyond the*
    *you of the world that is*
    *admired and known by others;*
*a "you" which is especially mine;*
*which cannot ever change,*
*and which I cannot ever*
    *cease to love.*

            *— Guy de Maupassant*

*So often, when I'm alone with my thoughts,*
*I feel your presence enter me*
*like the morning sun's early light,*
*filling my memories and dreams of us*
*with a warm and clear radiance.*
*You have become my love, my life,*
*and together we have shaped our world*
*until it seems now as natural as breathing.*
*But I remember when it wasn't always so —*
*times when peace and happiness seemed more*
*like intruders in my life than*
*the familiar companions they are today;*
*times when we struggled to know each other,*
*but always smoothing out those rough spots*
*until we came to share ourselves completely.*
*We can never rid our lives entirely*
*of sadness and difficult times — but we*
*can understand them together, and grow*
*stronger as individuals and as a loving couple.*
*If I don't tell you as often as I'd like,*
*it's because I could never tell you enough —*
*that I'm grateful for you*
*sharing your life with mine,*
*and that my love for you will live forever.*

— *Edmund O'Neill*

*I* know you care.
I can see it
　in your eyes.
I know you love me;
　you so often tell me.

You must know that
it's hard to express
all the tender emotion
　I feel in my heart for you.

It's there.
Every day,
　every night,
　　every second of the hour,
every day of the year.

And in the years to come,
I pray that
we will always mean
　this much
　　to each other.

— Sheri Daugherty

Are you afraid of my love?
...do not be frightened.
My love will not bind you.
It will bring warmth
    when you are cold,
    and companionship when you are lonely.
My love will bring smiles
    to brighten all your days,
    and understanding when you are sad.
It will not obligate you...
For my love will trust you always.
My love will give you all these things,
Asking only that
Wherever you go
And whatever you do,
You will hold me in your heart,
Knowing that when you return
I will be here...
To make you happy.

— Nancy Sue Krenrich

*By letting go of some*
*of your fears about love*
*and showing me the emotions*
*that once you were so*
*afraid of,*
*you've enabled me to feel*
*closer to you*
*than I've ever felt before.*
*I am happy*
*and I hope you will*
*always remember*
*that needing someone isn't*
*a sign of weakness,*
*but rather,*
*a sign of love.*

*— Tracy L. Trainer*

# To come home
# to you...

People always say things like,
"Do you ever feel like getting away
from it all?" Away from the worries of
the rush-about days that always
   seem to be?
I know that I do...
I need something in my life
that is solid and secure
and someplace that I can escape to —
where I can close out any worries
and open up to more peaceful things.

I'm luckier than a lot of people, I guess —
for I have found someplace I can go
where my heart is always happy to be
and where I have someone I can turn to,
someone who is an essential
part of me.

And the best part of all
   is that all I have to do...
      is just come home to you.

                      — Jamie Delere

*Because of you...*
*I've stopped running away*
*from love;*
*I no longer want to live*
*inside myself.*
*I want to live within you,*
*to respond to you and*
*to grow from your response*
*to me.*
*I never want to shut you*
*out of my life because*
*you are the best thing*
*that's ever happened*
*to me.*

— *Edward O'Blenis*

# I give you my love...

*For the harmony you bring into*
  *my life...*
*I give you my love*
*For the understanding of my needs*
*and the many smiles you have*
  *brought to me...*
*I give you my love*
*For the joy you bring to my heart*
*and the many ways you make me feel*
  *with every embrace...*
*I give you my love*
*For the comfort you bring to me*
*and the many treasured times*
  *we have shared...*
*I give you my love*
*For the way you are my friend*
*as well as the many ways you*
  *express our love...*
*I give you my love*
*For the many ways that you've*
  *allowed me to be a part of*
  *your life...*
*I give you my love*

*— Richard W. Weber*

Why is it that
When we are together
Time seems to fly,
And when we are apart
It drags so?
Could it be that
The passing of time
Is directly related to
The nearness
Of you?

— Thomas R. Dudley

*The moment we part*
*I begin to anticipate*
   *the next time*
*we'll be together...*
*laughing and sharing.*

*Each hour, each day*
*seems like forever.*
*The in-betweens of our*
   *togetherness*
*become harder to bear,*
*as my love for you*
   *grows*
      *stronger.*

— *Margaret O'Reilly-Lahda*

*I think of you*
    *so often.*
*You keep dropping by my mind.*
*I think of you*
*at the oddest times*
    *and in the strangest places.*
*How nice it feels*
*to be constantly surprised*
*by beautiful thoughts*
    *of you.*

— Claudia Adrienne Grandi

# *Just between you and me...*

*I want our love to always be a*
    *personal thing —*
*just between you and me.*
*There will be others who will*
    *think they know us better*
*than we know ourselves —*
*who will want to offer their*
    *opinions*
*on the way we ought to be*
*There will be times when we*
    *are curious or confused*
*and we'll find comfort in*
    *talking to a friend*
*or spending time alone...*

*But if ever there is a problem*
    *involving the two of us,*
*I hope that we will always come*
    *to each other first,*
*For just as it took only the two*
    *of us to fall in love,*
*the two of us can overcome*
    *any obstacle*
*that ever gets in the way.*

*— Lindsay Newman*

When I think of love —
I think of a sweet smile,
   a tender gaze,
   a gentle touch.

When I think of love,
I think of picnics,
   walks in the park,
   watching a sunset.

When I think of love,
I think of hope,
   togetherness,
   and sharing.

When I think of love,
I think of the simple things
   and you.

— Janice C. Sullivan

*I* have always sought gentleness
in my relationships

it gives me rest
from the barriers that surround me

it gives me peace
from the constant wrestling
of whether or not
I should just be myself

I tire of deciding if
I should let someone know
the intimate side of me
or if I should smile
or simply touch the hand of
a friend

Thank you for your warmth
it gives me pleasure
to have truly found
a gentle person

— Sharon T. Salter

*I sometimes feel*
*a little jealous in my thoughts,*
*imagining that someone else*
*could please you more than me.*
*It's just my insecurity*
*acting up a bit, I guess...*
*because I know I'm not*
  *the most beautiful,*
  *the most enticing,*
  *the most fun, or the*
  *most imaginative person*
    *in the world,*
*but I do know this —*
*no matter*
*how much time goes by,*
*I can't imagine that*
*you'll ever find another*
*who will love you*
*with a beauty*
  *and a passion*
    *and a happiness*
*like that which I feel for you.*

— *Laine Parsons*

# We'll be okay, won't we?

The one thing that matters
more to me than anything else
    in the world… is you and me.
You are my world.
You're the one who gets all
    my love and my wishes and my prayers.
But somehow… despite all my
    best intentions,
I never feel quite safe enough
    or sure enough
to rest assured that I'll always be
able to make you happy.

*I need to know.*
*I need you more than my words can say.*
*I need to always feel*
    *the warm peaceful feeling*
    *that I get when you hold me.*
*I need to experience the beauty*
    *of our love that I gently receive*
        *when we caress.*

*I need for us to remember*
    *all the love that's been given*
    *and all the love that will unfold*
    *each day, between the wonder of you*
        *and the warmth of me.*

*And sometimes,*
    *I just need to know*
        *that we'll be okay... won't we?*

— *Jamie Delere*

# A special thought...

*Sometimes it's not enough just to have you in my life; there are times when I need more of you than you give — more attention, more understanding, maybe even a little more of your time. Please understand. I don't want to crowd you or ask too much. I guess that I just want you to open up a little bit more... share more of your thoughts with me, your feelings and fears.*

*But most of all,*
*I want you to always remember...*

*that you can trust me with your love, and I want you to know that the more of you that you can give, the more of me you'll see smiling... with the wish to give nothing but good things back to you.*

*— Laine Parsons*

# You Are the Love of My Life

You show me you love me by your commitment to me. Your actions speak the truth and they agree with the words you say to me. Your expressions tell me your feelings. You define your love for me by the way you treat me. You're the person who shares my purpose in life and helps define my happiness. You are the one in whom all my dreams and hopes and plans are committed.

In our private world, we talk about things no one else will ever hear. No one but you will ever know this place with me, and I will never know this place with anyone else but you. Although things are not always perfect between us, we know that our love will always help us find a way to work things out together and it will grow stronger over time.

*I am thankful for our blessed relationship.*
*We are together in every way. Our love is*
*not a place we came to and left. We stayed.*
*It is not something that will go out of style*
*or that we feel just for today or tomorrow.*
*It is not dependent on any conditions.*

*To us, our love means forever and no matter*
*what, and because of our faithfulness, we*
*have a sacred trust.*

*I believe in our love. It not only fills our*
*present and our future, but it creates our*
*destiny together. We are soul mates, lovers,*
*and friends, and you are the love of my life.*

— *Donna Fargo*

When we first met
I held back so much
afraid to show my deepest feelings
As I got to know you better
your gentleness and honesty
encouraged me to open up
and I started a trust
in you that I never had
with anyone else
Once I started to express
my feelings
I realized that
this is the only way
to have a relationship
It is such a
wonderful feeling
to let myself
be completely known to you
Thank you
so much
for showing me
what two people can
share together
I look forward to
spending many beautiful
times with you

— Susan Polis Schutz

# I Give My Love
# to You Only

*I* want
to live and love with you
and be one forever;
to be near you so I can
reach out and touch you;
to make love with you,
talk with you,
and be silent with you;
to hold you close every night
and wake up with you
each morning.

I want
to share my secrets with you
and be honest with you;
to understand and respect you,
accepting you as you are.

*I want*
*to find shelter in you*
  *when I am afraid*
*and hold you when I need warmth;*
*to be with you through all seasons,*
*walking with you in the sunshine*
*and cuddling with you in the cold.*

*I want*
*to care for you when you are ill*
*and be joyful with you when you*
  *are happy;*
*to grow old with you*
*and be with you until*
  *the end of time.*
*I want all these things*
  *with you only.*
*I would do all these things*
  *for you only.*
*To you only, I give all my love.*

— *Jacqueline Faye Sanderson-Mixon*

# I Love Having You to Love

You are my one true love.
The days we share are my blessings.
The memories we make are my treasures.
The togetherness we have is
    my dream come true.
And the understanding we share is
    something I've never had
        with anyone but you.
If anyone ever asked me
what part of my life you are...
    I would just have to
    look at them and smile
and say, "The <u>best</u> part."

The happiness you give to me
is something I'll never
    be able to get enough of.

I love having you in my world.

    And I love
        having you
            to love.

— *Chris Gallatin*

# ACKNOWLEDGMENTS

*The following is a partial list of authors whom the publisher especially wishes to thank for permission to reprint their works.*

*Michael J. Mulvena for "What I wanted when I first...." Copyright © 1983 by Michael J. Mulvena. Karen Jessie for "To you my love, I vow...." Copyright © 1983 by Karen Jessie. Sheri Daugherty for "I know you care." Copyright © 1983 by Sheri Daugherty. Nancy Sue Krenrich for "Are you afraid of my love?" Copyright © 1983 by Nancy Sue Krenrich. Tracy L. Trainer for "By letting go of some of your fears...." Copyright © 1983 by Tracy L. Trainer. Edward O'Blenis for "Because of you...." Copyright © 1983 by Edward O'Blenis. Richard W. Weber for "I give you my love...." Copyright © 1983 by Richard W. Weber. Thomas R. Dudley for "Why is it that...." Copyright © 1983 by Thomas R. Dudley. Margaret O'Reilly-Lahda for "The moment we part...." Copyright © 1983 by Margaret O'Reilly-Lahda. Claudia Adrienne Grandi for "I think of you so often." Copyright © 1983 by Claudia Adrienne Grandi. Janice C. Sullivan for "When I think of love...." Copyright © 1983 by Janice C. Sullivan. Sharon T. Salter for "I have always sought gentleness...." Copyright © 1983 by Sharon T. Salter. PrimaDonna Entertainment Corp. for "You Are the Love of My Life" by Donna Fargo. Copyright © 2000 by PrimaDonna Entertainment Corp. All rights reserved.*

*The following works have previously appeared in Blue Mountain Arts® publications:*

*"You have my love for..." by Daniel Haughian. Copyright © 1983 by Daniel Haughian. All rights reserved.*

*"I'm not sure when I first...," "I want nothing but the best...," "To come home to you...," and "We'll be okay, won't we?" by Jamie Delere, "Our first times are...," "Touched by Love," and "Just between you and me..." by Lindsay Newman, "You and I took a special chance..." and "So often, when I'm alone..." by Edmund O'Neill, "I sometimes feel..." and "A special thought..." by Laine Parsons, "To someone who is beautiful..." by Andrew Tawney, "I Love Having You to Love" by Chris Gallatin, "I Give My Love to You Only" by Jacqueline Faye Sanderson-Mixon, "What It's like to Love You" by Daniel Haughian, and "'You'" by Anna Tafoya. Copyright © 1983, 1984, 1991, 1995, and 1998 by SPS Studios, Inc. All rights reserved.*

*A careful effort has been made to trace the ownership of poems used in this anthology in order to obtain permission to reprint copyrighted materials and give proper credit to the copyright owners. If any error or omission has occurred, it is completely inadvertent, and we would like to make corrections in future editions provided that written notification is made to the publisher:*

SPS STUDIOS, INC.
P.O. Box 4549, Boulder, Colorado 80306.